Treasures Old & New

Treasures
Old &
New

Wesleyan Faith
for Life Today

Michael Adam Beck &
Steve Harper

Abingdon Press

Nashville

Contents

Introduction

JESUS'S CENTRAL MESSAGE was the reign of God. He compared it to a treasure. He said that those who are trained to advance it will bring "old and new things out of their treasure chest" (Matthew 13:52 CEB). We believe this is an essential combination if renewal is to occur. If we only repeat the old ways, we will be obscurantists. If we only create new ways, we will be rootless. The way forward calls for a conjoining of the two.

The Wesleys and the early Methodist movement are models for doing this. They combined a commitment to primitive Christianity with a desire to "serve the present age." They brought forth treasures old and new, offering

Christ in ways that reached the marginalized, renewed the church, and reformed the nation.

Renewal envisions and enacts a weaving together of the past and present. In this book we write about this vision. Steve writes the chapter portions about the old treasures of the Wesleyan tradition, and Michael writes about the new treasures being offered through fresh expressions of faith and ministry. We do not view our respective work as separate. We each know something about the other's portion. In fact, we have read and provided input into all of the work.

At the same time, we acknowledge that our ministries have located us in different places in the renewal effort. We hope that writing from our respective vantage points means we come to the table offering you our strengths born of study and experience.

Taking this approach, we believe we represent the spirit of the Wesleys and the substance of early Methodism. It was a movement long before it was a denomination. But John and Charles knew that movements build upon the past. Otherwise, they cannot be sustained. Calling early Methodism a manifestation of "Scriptural Christianity" was their way of uniting the past and present.

We have written a shorter book intentionally, pointing to selected primary treasures, old and new. The footnotes and reading list will take you further in your study.

We see this book as an invitation to you to engage yourself in renewal. Some of you may do it more in terms of the older treasures; others of you may contribute new treasures. Both are necessary.

Brandan Robertson, a young Christian leader, has written about the necessity of old treasures, pointing out that "finding very little to grab a hold of, very little sense of rootedness and grounding, can even lead to many people walking away from this movement, feeling that it is shallow and lifeless."[1]

Lisa Sharon Harper writes about new treasures, reminding us that the gospel writers "all cared about an individual's reconciliation with God, self, and their communities. But [they] also focused on systemic justice, peace between people groups, and freedom for the oppressed. The good news was both about the coming of the Kingdom of God and the character of that Kingdom. It was about what God's Kingdom looked like. It was about what citizenship in God's Kingdom requires. The biblical gospel writers' good news was about the restoration of shalom."[2]

We see the blend of past and present in the Covenant Renewal Service of early Methodism. Based in lit-

---

1. Brandan Robertson, "Reclaiming Our Progressive Christian Tradition," *Progressing Spirit* eletter, July 27, 2023.

2. Lisa Sharon Harper, *The Very Good Gospel* (WaterBrook, 2016), 6.

urgy that exhibited the best of the Christian tradition, the service itself aimed to rekindle the flame of devotion in the coming year. Participants pledged themselves to live for Christ through the "many services to be done" in the church and the world.

Our hope is that by teaming up to write about this treasured renewal, we will inspire you to join with others in the same work.

Michael Beck
Steve Harper

The Mindset

An Old Treasure

One of John Wesley's early writings was *The Character of a Methodist* (1742). The way he wrote it was masterful and important. He described a particular expression of Christianity (Methodism) without disconnecting it from the larger reality.[1]

---

1. *The Character of a Methodist* is available in its original form in a variety of versions. An inexpensive eBook edition is available from Amazon. The standard and substantive edition (text and notes) is found in *The Works of John Wesley*, Volume 9: The Methodist Societies, edited by Rupert E. Davies (Abingdon Press, 1989).

He achieved this in two ways. First, he chose to identify Methodists using universal Christian descriptions. He wrote that a Methodist loves God and others (grounding Methodism in the two great commandments), and that a Methodist rejoices in God, gives thanks, and prays constantly.[2]

Second, he ended the treatise making it clear that Methodists are, and are intended to be, nothing other than genuine Christians. He put it this way, "By these marks, by these fruits of a living faith, we do labour to distinguish ourselves from the unbelieving world. . . . But from real Christians, of whatever denominations they be, we earnestly desire not to be distinguished at all."[3]

In *The Character of a Methodist,* we find our mindset. It is one of traditioning. When rightly practiced, we make disciples, not members. But we do so through the lens of our particular expression of faith. This is not anything unusual or new.

Life abundant is formed through concrete means.

When we want to get inside a building, we do so through one door. When we want to drive a car, we rent

---

2. Steve's book, *Five Marks of a Methodist* (Abingdon Press, 2015) is a contemporary re-presentation of Wesley's original work, aiming to establish the same marks in Methodists today.

3. *The Works of Wesley,* volume 9, 42.

or purchase a specific brand. When we desire to further our education, we enroll in a certain school. The same holds true in our spiritual formation. We experience the universal in the particular. None of this is exclusivism, but only our recognition that life abundant is formed through concrete means. Jesus described it as having wineskins or jars to hold God's wine. Containers are necessary, just not primary.

The Wesleys understood this and designed Methodism accordingly. They kept the marks of a Methodist based in Scriptural Christianity, but they offered people Christ through a (then) new wineskin (fresh expression) called Methodism.

We are living in a time of "do it yourself" religion blended with a high distrust of institutional Christianity. More than disaffiliations or church closures, the current societal skepticism is eroding much of what we have included in the word *church*. The outcome of this remains to be seen, but one thing is clear: business as usual will not suffice.

God is once again doing a new thing (Isaiah 43:19 CEB), and the prophet's question is, "Don't you recognize it?" Recognition is a mindset—what Jesus called having seeing eyes and hearing ears (Mark 8:18).

The traditioning mindset helps people establish and enrich their identity: Christian disciples. This means keeping the christological core in view and in play. It is forming people into the mind that was in Christ (Philippians 2:5-8). From Paul's words we learn that Christ-likeness includes humility, consecration, servanthood, obedience, and sacrifice.

From this identity, the additional components named in this book emerge. In short, Christianity is life in Christ.[4] The Wesleys knew this, and they designed Methodism to represent and nurture the vision.

Applied to today, we seek to establish in ourselves the mindset that keeps us one with others, eschewing partisanship and embracing ecumenicity. At the same time, we believe that the Wesleyan tradition is a good lens through which to see real Christianity. We offer people Christ with this mindset.

A New Treasure

The Wesleys missional mindset was also what we would call today a "futuring" mindset. Their primary concern was the vast sea of people who had no connection with the church and likely never would in its current form. They sought to discern and interpret societal-ecclesial trends and iterate forward toward multiple plausible

---

4. Steve develops this further in his book, *Life in Christ: The Core of Intentional Spirituality* (Abingdon Press, 2020).

alternatives. While "innovation" had a primarily negative connotation in their day, for all intents and purposes they were innovating new forms of Chirstian community, cobbling together a "practical divinity" as they engaged in the process of mission.

Two words came about primarily to describe the Methodist way: "doctrine and discipline." The doctrine of early Methodists was grounded in a grace-centered all-encompassing view of God's mission to heal all people and all the world. Discipline referred to the practical social constructs to facilitate that mission.

Perhaps this synthesis, and a commitment to renewal from within, is the most Methodist thing of all.

As treasured-renewal people, early Methodists experimented with wild new forms of communal life in Jesus while remaining tethered to the inherited Anglican Church. Perhaps this synthesis, and a commitment to renewal from within, is the most Methodist thing of all.

Returning to Jesus's metaphor about new and old wineskins, as structures and delivery vehicles for the good news that is for all people, it's easy to skip over the detail in Matthew's version, "But new wine is put into fresh wineskins, *and so both are preserved*" (Matthew 9:17 NRSVue, italics ours). We need both the vintage and the fresh, with both forms being equally important. In Luke's version,

Jesus even indicates the old vintage stuff is to be preferred, "And no one after drinking old wine wants the new, for they say, 'The old is better'" (Luke 5:39 NIV).

I (Michael) have been experimenting with fresh expressions over the past seventeen years. As a person who has lived more on the new wineskin side of things, I can say I have seen the problems when this both/and mindset is not present, and the fruitfulness when it is. There is a tendency among those more apostolically minded among us to dismiss and even abandon the old treasures, to burn down the house of tradition. Something in our wiring makes the tendency feel natural as we keep our eyes focused on the ones that aren't here yet. But this is an instinct we must resist.

> A new treasure that is not combined with the old treasure of tradition will eventually die.

A new treasure that is not combined with the old treasure of tradition will eventually die. In the words of Jesus, "apart from me you can do nothing" (John 15:5 NRSVue), and to use one of Paul's favorite phrases, to be "in Christ" is to be baptized into a community.[5] In

---

5. A variation of the expression "in Christ" occurs 216 times in Paul's writings and 26 times in the Johannine literature. It is an essential idea in the early church and is found (in different variations) in every major Christian theological tradition.

John 15, the key word is "abide" in Jesus. This involves at least three dimensions of mutual indwelling: Christ is inhabiting us ("Christian"), we are inhabiting Christ ("in Christ"), and a community of disciples is indwelled by the Risen Jesus ("the church"). We are connected to a vine of many branches and rooted in a tradition that spans back thousands of years. Yes, there are parts of the vine that are sick and need healing, but we are living in an illusion if we think there is a "churchless Christianity" that can live apart from tradition.

For example, some of the healthiest and most fruitful Fresh Expressions of Church across the globe are those that spring up out of their tradition, not in opposition to it. These new-treasure practitioners have found a way to anchor radical change in deep values.[6] They are reclaiming a core part of their tradition's story that seems to have been lost for a time.

While Fresh Expressions is an ecumenical movement that transcends any single tradition, it is also one of the most Methodist things in the world today. Perhaps even more so, in terms of early Methodism, as it has re-awakened versions of field preaching, an utter seriousness around holiness (as love of God and neighbor), an understanding of waves of grace that happen in a series of social constructs (society, class, band), and the inclu-

---

6. See Ken Carter and Michael Beck, *Gardens in the Desert* (Abingdon, 2024) for more on these ideas.

sive nature of early Methodism that sought to be "friends to all."[7]

So, as I progress forward in the new-treasure sections, I want to emphasize this connection but move further into the lived-theology parts—the "practical divinity" aspects. A guiding question will be, "What are the new treasures we see being offered by Christ followers in the twenty-first century?"

---

7. Laceye Warner reminds us that John Wesley was particularly proud of the inclusive nature of Methodist societies who would "admit anyone." Laceye Warner, *Knowing Who We Are* (Abingdon Press, 2024), 17, 28.

The Message

An Old Treasure

The heart of our message is love, simply because this is the essence of biblical revelation. The Gospel begins, continues, and ends in love. Paul Chilcote captured this truth when he wrote, "The Wesleys' intent was not to create a doctrinal system to believe in, but to inspire a life of love to live in."[1]

---

1. Paul W. Chilcote, *Multiplying Love* (Abingdon Press, 2023).

Ours is a theology of love. Mildred Bangs Wynkoop helped many of us see this when she wrote, *A Theology of Love: The Dynamic of Wesleyanism.*[2] She took readers into the writings and hymnody of the Wesleys, which themselves lead us into Scripture and tradition. Love is the message that created and sustained Christianity. It is the message that will revive and mature us.

> Jesus's life and ministry was a fulfilling, a refilling, a full filling of what had been lost—the ingredient of love.

We begin by noting Jesus's words that he did not come to destroy the law but to fulfill it. The Greek word translated *fulfill* indicates that the law had been drained of something it once had and needed to have again. Jesus's life and ministry was a fulfilling, a refilling, a full filling of what had been lost—the ingredient of love. The law apart from love became legalism. Jesus would not let that continue.

Neither must we. Sadly, we are living in a time when some Christians advance legalism more than love. Of course, they deny this. But to use Jesus's words, by their fruits you shall know them, and theirs is waxed fruit. All

2. Mildred Bangs Wynkoop, *A Theology of Love: The Dynamic of Wesleyanism* (Beacon Hill, 1972). In 2015, it was republished in a second edition that contains tribute articles to her.

we have to do is to ask the "nones" why they keep their distance from Christianity or inquire of the "dones" why they have walked away from it, and in less than a minute they will couch their decision in relation to a lack of love in the church.

We have our marching orders. We must establish our message in love. But what does that mean? The word *love* has become so counterfeited, caricatured, and compromised as to be as drained of its meaning in our day as the law had been emptied of love in Jesus's day. To even speak of our message as one of love requires us to identify some key aspects of love we are called to live.

The first aspect is love that is inherent in God's nature. God is love (1 John 4:8). The Bible uses different words to describe God's love.[3] Thomas Oord sums it up in the phrase *pluriform love*.[4] God is with us in multiple expressions of never-failing love—that is, God is disposed to love us in whatever ways we need to be loved, and to do this in time, and for eternity. The new creation toward which we are moving is the culmination of God's love.

The second aspect of love is expressed in God's action. We call this *grace*. The Wesleys described the way of salvation in relation to grace: prevenient, converting,

---

3. Some of the key ones are *ahavah, rachamim, hesed, eros, phileo, storge,* and *agape.*
4. Thomas Jay Oord, *Pluriform Love* (SacraSage, 2022).

sanctifying, and glorifying.[5] They preached, taught, and sang their way through the story of grace.[6] And just as the Bible does, they went on to declare that in the economy of grace, God gives us the will and the means to love as God's loves.[7] Because we have first been loved by God, we then love others.

The third aspect of love is manifested in God's inclusion. God loves the world (John 3:16), is unwilling that any should perish (2 Peter 3:9), and accomplishes this desire through Christ (1 Corinthians 15:22). The dividing wall is broken down; all are one in Christ (Ephesians 2:14, Galatians 3:28). In the new creation this is confirmed by the innumerable host from every tribe and nation (Revelation 7:9).

To see love in God's nature, actions, and inclusion does not fully describe a theology of love. But it is sufficient to confirm that our core message is love. We have

---

5. We use the term *converting grace* intentionally. It preserves the Wesleyan union of justifying and regenerating grace, which sometimes is lost when the two concepts are treated separately. Converting grace is the simultaneous action of God for us (justification) and in us (regeneration). Justification, John Wesley said, is a relative change; regeneration is a real change. Steve writes more about this in *The Way to Heaven* (Zondervan, 2003).

6. Randy Maddox, *Responsible Grace* (Kingswood Books, 1994). Paul Chilcote makes the same point in his book, *A Faith That Sings* (Cascade Books, 2016).

7. Roberta Bondi, *To Love as God Loves* (Fortress, 1987).

a moment to tell others who wonder if God loves them and if the Church does too that they are God's beloved, now and always.

A New Treasure

In order to love we have to care. Love takes proximity, time, commitment, and healthy communication habits. It requires caring enough about people to be with them, to listen, to learn, and to make sacrifices of our time. Law is neat. Love is messy. It doesn't happen in the hurried, commoditized, and transactional way of modern society.

On May 3, 2023, United States Surgeon General Dr. Vivek Murthy released an advisory titled "Our Epidemic of Loneliness and Isolation." The report details the rise of this epidemic and describes the healing effects of social connection and community.[8] While we have never been more connected, thanks to technology, we have never been more alone. The epidemic of isolation had led to a rise in depression, suicide, substance abuse, and overdose deaths. People die of loneliness every day.

---

8. Public Health Service. Office of the Surgeon General, "Our Epidemic of Loneliness and Isolation," U.S. Department of Health and Human Services (HHS), 2023. Accessed May 5, 2023.

What a tragedy, being that the church has one unique gift that can heal the world—communal life in Jesus. The church is to be a community of unconditional love. A *koinonia* community where every person can be known, loved, and supported through every facet of life. A community where people can think differently, vote differently, and massively disagree on many things, and yet what unites us together makes all of those differences seem small.

The message of love is inextricably linked to the mode of its presentation. Or as Canadian philosopher and technological prophet Marshall McLuhan first famously said, "The medium is the message."[9] That is no more profoundly true than in the Gospel of Jesus Christ. The message? The God of love, in the fullness of time, put on flesh to get to us and love us into wholeness. "The Word became flesh and blood, and moved into the neighborhood" (John 1:14, The Message).

Jesus is the embodiment of the love of God. Theologians have described this mystery with the word *incarnation*. The Late Latin *incarnari* "be made flesh," from "in" and "carnis" provides a deeper meaning, like the word became a piece of meat.

Jesus cares enough to enter our daily lives and rhythms. There is proximity, time, commitment, and

---

9. Marshall McLuhan and W. T. Gordon, *Understanding Media: The Extensions of Man* (Gingko Press, 2003), 9.

healthy communication. His life was the substance of his message: a life of love, manifested for our own well-being and wholeness. One of the repeated words that describes the inner motivation of Jesus is *compassion*.

Matthew 9:36 reports that when Jesus "saw the crowds, he had compassion for them because they were harassed and helpless, like sheep without a shepherd." The Greek word translated compassion, *splanchnizomai*, means to be moved as to one's bowels, hence, to be moved with compassion. The bowels were thought to be the seat of love and mercy. So Jesus has a gut-wrenching love that inspires him to act.

Compassion can be described as a sensitivity to suffering in self and others with a commitment to try to alleviate and prevent it. The Gospels articulate the architecture of Jesus's compassion, which gives us a window into the heart of God.

The church as the "body of Christ" (1 Corinthians 12:27) in the world is an expression of Christ's own compassion. An active, practical, inclusive love should emanate endlessly from the church.

For Christians, compassion is not mere emotionality but rather a new mode of being, empowered by the Spirit. This involves embodying not just the *truth* and *life* of Jesus but following the actual *way* of Jesus (John 14:16).

The first Methodists didn't wait for people to come hear the message of love. They moved out into the fields,

They formed communities with people outside the inherited church spaces, in small groups that could meet anywhere.

sharing it freely with all who would listen. They formed communities with people outside the inherited church spaces, in small groups that could meet anywhere. Early Methodism was incarnational and compassion-centered.

This is a primary value in Fresh Expressions of Church. We don't wait back at the church compound for people to show up. Because we care about our neighbors, we gather with them in the normal everyday spaces of life. Sociologist Ray Oldenburg provides helpful language to describe these spaces as first place (home), second place (work), and third place (common neutral spaces, parks, coffee shops, pubs, restaurants, tattoo parlors, etc.).[10]

Our commitment is to embody the message of love in communities that are inclusive and accessible (more on these values later). We offer these treasures in all kinds of settings, at all kinds of times, and around all kinds of practices. Because we are committed to living a message of love whenever and wherever our neighbor invites us.

---

10. Ray Oldenburg, *The Great Good Place: Cafés, Coffee Shops, Bookstores, Bars, Hair Salons, and Other Hangouts at the Heart of a Community* (Marlowe, 1999).

The Movement

An Old Treasure

As long as the Wesleys were alive, Methodism was more a movement than an organization. Our tradition exhibits a movement mentality. As a denomination, we cannot fully replicate that, but we can connect with the spirit of it. It is important for us to do so.

For one thing, it calls us to the accept the fact that "the system" is not the solution. A movement mentality is not anti-institutional; it just refuses to make the institution paramount. A movement mentality blends theology and sociology in ways that keep the Church organic. This enables us to hold things loosely while not rejecting them outright.

For another thing, a movement mentality is subversive—an additional quality that appeals to many today.[1] In the days of early Methodism, this was termed an "ecclesiola en ecclesia"—a little church within the big Church. But not in a passive way but rather as an active presence aimed at renewal. Methodism was clearly that, and the institutionalists did not like it. They still don't. The sacred-cow feeders pushed back on the Wesleys. They still push back on people like them.

But they persevered, and so must we. It is a movement mentality that inspires and strengthens us to endure. It offers us gifts for doing so.

First, it connects us with God's intention to do new things (Isaiah 43:19). We are not in the prison named "We've never done it that way before." We are free to be Pentecost people who dream dreams and see visions (Acts 2:17). In ways akin to our Buddhist friends, we recognize the impermanence of all things, even as Jesus did (Matthew 24:2). Innovation is in play when we have a movement mentality.

Second, it confirms Christianity's need for new wineskins. This is another way to speak of imperma-

---

1. Eugene Peterson points to the significance of this in his book, *Subversive Spirituality* (Eerdmans, 1997).

nence, but it does so with a specific metaphor. No matter how good a wineskin may be, it will eventually become brittle and leak. People with a movement mentality recognize this. Emergence Christianity has been on the forefront of this recognition for some time.[2] We have much to learn from this movement.

Third, it calls forth a creative synthesis of the past and the present. Movement people are not obscurantists. They welcome the contributions made by our predecessors in the faith; they just don't worship them or believe they have the final word on things. Movement people believe in progressive revelation and seek to be what Jesus called someone "who brings old and new things out of their treasure chest" (Matthew 13:52 CEB).

Fourth, it creates a locality. The kingdom of God is near, at hand. A movement mentality unites vocation and location, urging us to live here-and-now. Eugene Peterson believed we do this when we ask the question, "Who are these particular people, and how can I be with them in such a way that they can become what God is making them?"[3] Will Willimon amplifies the idea when he writes, "The Holy Spirit is God going local."[4]

---

2.   Phyllis Tickle, *Emergence Christianity* (Baker Books, 2012).

3.   Eugene Peterson, *The Contemplative Pastor* (Word Publishing, 1989), 11.

4.   Will Willimon, *Don't Look Back* (Abingdon Press, 2022), x.

Fifth, a movement mentality constructs ministry networks. No single entity is expected to be a full-service ministry. Paul's phrase about the gifts of the spirit, "to each is given," characterizes how ministry gets done. Partnerships with religious and civic organizations weave a tapestry of results without any one thread doing it all. In a time of institutional decline, networking is essential. People with a movement mentality affirm, celebrate, and create networks. They enact ecumenism.

> People with a movement mentality affirm, celebrate, and create networks.

Early Methodism was expressive of a movement mentality in each of these ways and more.[5] When we combine these things, they become one word: simplicity.[6] And they enable us to travel light.[7] Grounding ourselves in a movement mentality is a rest from having to keep the plates spinning—and it is a reliance upon God's power more than our own to get things done (Zechariah 4:6).

---

5. The reading list's referencing of books by George Hunter, Gil Rendle, and Leonard Sweet expand the idea of Methodism as a movement.

6. Richard Foster, *Freedom of Simplicity*, Revised and Updated (HarperCollins, 2005).

7. Eugene Peterson, *Traveling Light* (Helmers & Howard, 1988).

A New Treasure

Jesus sends the disciples out two by two with instructions to travel light: "Carry no purse, no bag, no sandals, and greet no one on the road." The disciples were not constructing buildings and playing host. Hospitality of this variety was not part of their training. Jesus was teaching them to be good guests: "Whatever house you enter, first say, 'Peace to this house!' And if a person of peace is there, your peace will rest on that person, but if not, it will return to you" (Luke 10:4-6 NRSVue).

Luke 10:1-9 is an essential text for a movement mindset people. In some ways it is our blueprint for being church in the way of Jesus, a treasure for fresh expressions and other new ways of being the body of Christ. It is not a stationary way of life; it is movemental. We are sent out into the world, looking for "persons of peace." We are dependent on the hospitality of the ones we are sent to. This is both at once a posture of vulnerability and mutuality. The hospitality of our hosts can be fickle. Rejection is a possibility. We come mostly empty-handed, bringing the gift of withness but not much else.

This way of being has been recapitulated by every third-order movement across history. It stands in stark contrast to the stationary and attractional-only way of church. In that mode, we build a structure, stick up a sign, invite people to come on our terms, at a time we have chosen, to worship in a way we have determined. It requires no vulnerability on our part. And there is no mutuality: we have everything our guests need, all they have to do is show up and leave a tip in the bucket.

However, we "have built it and they have not come." People are suspicious of our hospitality. The greatest tragedies of Christian history have occurred when Christians found themselves in the center of power, wealth, and the ability to enforce our will with violence. This led to holy wars, inquisitions, witch trials, and the justification of slavery, to name a few.

Can the movemental church show the institution a new way? Can Jerusalem (old-treasure, fixed, attractional) learn to live in symbiotic relationship with Antioch (new-treasure, mobile, sent) like what we see in Acts 15?

Consider the thousands of fresh expressions now dotting the landscape of the post-Christendom West. If you focus in, they seem small, insignificant. A handful of people meeting in a living room, enjoying Asian food together, reading scripture to expose and heal from Asian American and Pacific Islander invisibility. A dozen folks in a burrito joint, dipping chips in a shared bowl of salsa, then lifting and breaking the tortilla, recounting the words of Jesus in the last supper. Thirty colorful out-casts, crowded around a coffee table sharing in a tattoo talk while the artist's gun hums in the background ink-ing Christian iconography on a canvas of flesh. A group of LBTQIA+ folk circled up in a coffee shop, healing from their church trauma one cup and one conversation at a time.

When you connect the dots of this network, it is vast, distributed, and unstoppable. These people seem to be doing something new, but they are drinking from ancient wells. Their relational web looks like the church in the first 300 years of her existence. Every once in a while, Ethiopians, Celtics, Benedictines, Beguines, and Methodists uncover those wells again so people discon-nected from the church can drink from the living water.

> These people seem to be doing something new, but they are drinking from ancient wells.

This doesn't mean movement is not stable, slow and steady, moving at the pace of grace or at the speed of relationship. Jesus did say, "Remain in the same house, eating and drinking whatever they provide. . . . Do not move about from house to house" (Luke 10:7 NRSVue). Doing life with people of peace requires commitment and time. It won't pander to our McDonaldized, fast-food, microwave relationships culture. There is no quick fix to knowing and loving one another in a deep way. And yet it is right there where we often discover healing for what ails us, and we can proclaim, "The kingdom of God has come near" (Luke 10:9 NRSVue).

The movement, after all, is the motion of love. The good news comes to us on the way to someone else. A heart strangely warmed at Aldersgate starts a fire in the field at Bristol. We cannot hold back the love of God, hoarding it to ourselves. We will start a house fire if we put the lamp under the bed or beneath the bushel basket. We have to carry it out to the hill, to light up the world.

The Method

An Old Treasure

We would expect that a movement named Methodism would exist and advance through a method. Initially used as a term of derision against the Wesleys and their companions at Oxford, John Wesley turned "Methodist" into one of the defining and directing words. Methodism was a movement with a method. In this chapter we will look at key aspects of it.

In a word, the method was *monastic*. In theology, the Methodists were a Matthew 6:33 people, seeking

The Wesleys mined monasticism, beginning with its expressions in early Christianity and moving ahead into their own day. They brought its treasures into the Methodist movement.

first the kingdom of God, with the singular devotion conveyed in the word *monk*. With this intention, the Wesleys mined monasticism, beginning with its expressions in early Christianity and moving ahead into their own day. They brought its treasures into the Methodist movement.

The monastic makeup of Methodism is one of the main studies I (Steve) have been engaged in over the years. I believe the Wesleys knew from where they were getting the bulk of their method, and that they saw Methodism as a new monasticism, a fresh expression of it.[1] From monasticism they gleaned life-giving principles and practices as they designed early Methodism.

Monasticism has been called "a school of love"[2] and "a school in the Lord's service."[3] The notion of a school

---

1. We have been helped by others who saw this before we did: Frank Baker, W. E. Sangster, Albert Outler, Martin Schmidt, Melvin Dieter, Colin Williams, Randy Maddox, Ted Campbell, Elaine Heath, and Paul Chilcote.

2. Basil Pennington, *A School of Love* (Morehouse Publishing, 2000).

3. A Cistercian description of monastic communities.

would itself have been attractive to the Wesleys, for whom discipleship formation was an orderly process.[4] When the ideas of love and service are added, the monastic model was a fit for early Methodism.

Furthermore, monasticism provided the foundational staff and documents. John was clearly the Abbot. And he provided a Constitution (*The Character of a Methodist*), a Rule (*The General Rules of the United Societies*), the formative pattern (the means of grace), a Conference that promoted the Connection (the Annual Conference), and a renewal experience (*The Covenant Renewal Service*).

All this came with the substance of the Benedictine order[5] and the spirit of the Franciscans.[6] Methodism was a Third-Order (non-cloistered) movement engaged in a variety of ministries expressed in a unified mission—both of which we will explore in upcoming chapters.

From a historical theology perspective, we note that monasticism has arisen both to preserve and promote

---

4. Theologically, the process followed the flow of grace, and sociologically, Methodism had a formative group corresponding to that flow: Prevenient Grace (the Societies), Converting Grace (the Classes), and Sanctifying Grace (the Bands, Penitent Bands, and Select Societies).

5. Paul W. Chilcote, *A Benedictine Wesleyan Way* (a book en route to publication at the time this book appears).

6. Frank Baker, Albert Outler, Colin Williams, and Ted Campbell (to name a few) have noted the influence of the Franciscan order upon early Methodism.

the Gospel. Monastics (those living with singular devotion to God) have kept the lights on and the fire burning when they might have otherwise gone out. Here is another way we see Methodism as a monastic movement.

The monastic roots of Methodism are especially important, for in the larger awakening taking place today, a New Monasticism is once again involved in it.[7] Methodism is right at home in this renewal.

A New Treasure

Fresh Expressions, as a new monastic movement, employs a method of spiritual formation that has deep resonance with early Methodism. As small, intentional communities, we are on a journey of healing in which we move through the waves of grace. With all seriousness, the focus of our communal life is to grow in love with God and neighbor. We want to experience union with Christ, and in so doing, we seek to become a people who think, act, and love more like him. A fruit of this pursuit is the embodiment of the compassion of Jesus in community with others.

7.   Jonathan Wilson-Hartgrove, *New Monasticism* (Brazos Press, 2008).

In our school of love, we follow a method called the "loving first journey." The movements of this journey are listening, loving and serving, building relationships, exploring discipleship, church taking shape, and repeating.

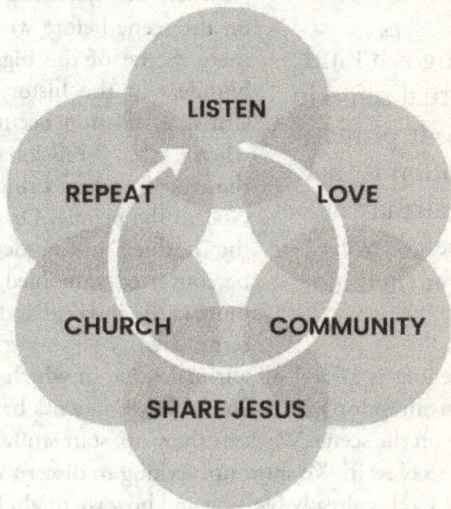

LISTEN

REPEAT   LOVE

CHURCH   COMMUNITY

SHARE JESUS

The first movement of the journey is listening. We remember that God gave us two ears and one mouth for a reason. We enter our community as learners. Our place is our teacher. We become students of the people. We are prayerfully listening to God and our context.

The Wesleyan emphasis on prevenient grace is essential here. We believe in a God who goes before us. There is no person we will ever encounter in whose life Jesus is not already involved. There is no place we will ever go where the Spirit was not on the scene before we got there. Some of the biggest blunders in the history of Christian mission occurred when the missionaries thought they were bringing God to the people. Or that the "heathen" just needed to be converted, ennobled, or, more sadly, enslaved and exterminated.

> Listening is a kind of spiritual sense in which our primary assumption is that God is already at work before we arrive on the scene.

Listening is a kind of spiritual sense in which our primary assumption is that God is already at work before we arrive on the scene. We don't show up, start stuff, and ask God to bless it. We show up, seeking to discern who and what God is already blessing and how we might join what God is up to. This is a spiritual practice that we cultivate over a lifetime.

As we are listening, we are looking for opportunities to love and serve our neighbor. Whereas many ideas of church begin with starting a worship service that we invite people to, we start with worshipful ser-

30

vice to our neighbors who have invited us into their lives. There is mutuality in this loving and serving; it is a two-way street. We have to unlearn the false assumption that we as Christians have all the answers and resources, and we just need to fix people's problems for them. We need the people to whom we are sent as much as they need us.

Every community has assets and opportunities. Sometimes we build relationships around exploring what those treasures are together. In other scenarios, there is obvious fragmentation in the community, an injustice that needs reparation, a wound that needs to be healed. We look to see where love is needed.

Our method resembles that of Jesus: he stood in the synagogue in Nazareth and read the social justice litany of the prophet Isaiah, "The Spirit of the Lord is upon me, because he has anointed me to bring good news to the poor. He has sent me to proclaim release to the captives and recovery of sight to the blind, to set free those who are oppressed, to proclaim the year of the Lord's favor" (Luke 4:18-19 NRSVue). Jesus then went about doing those very things, and as he did so, a group of disciples sprung up around him who would become the ongoing embodiment of his own life. Today, we are the extension of that embodiment.

So we start where Jesus started, with a desire to know and love our neighbor, to seek the common good

We start where Jesus started, with a desire to know and love our neighbor, to seek the common good of the people, to cultivate shalom.

of the people, to cultivate shalom. Sometimes this involves challenging systems of injustice, oppression, and exclusion. This method of love reintegrates social justice and the cultivation of new faith communities. The intrinsic motivation is love. There is no other agenda. As we love and serve one another in a spirit of mutuality, spiritual opportunities begin to open up. People begin to be transparent about their hopes, dreams, and struggles.

As the spirit of mutual love and service grows, a community often starts to form. We can start to be intentional about not just physical and emotional well-being, but spiritual as well. The community may include Christian and non-Christian people. We prioritize belonging over believing. In the community, we foster radical inclusivity, a space where people can find belonging, where they are known and loved. Believing comes at the pace of grace, or maybe never at all, but again the relationships are the mission.

Another helpful Wesleyan concept here is the idea of "awakening" to the grace of God that's already there. John Wesely would sometimes document how many people he assumed were awakened to the grace of God. It is in justifying grace that we step into that awareness. We respond to the wooing love of God in whatever way seems appropriate.

This can take many forms. Sometimes as we gather we simply ask a question like, "What spiritual practices are sustaining everyone right now?" or "What does your spiritual life look like?" We may introduce a poem or listen to a song from the playlist on our phone and then ask, "Did this resonate with anyone spiritually? If so, how?" It could be giving some instruction, setting a timer, and being still for a period of meditation.

When the Spirit nudges, and people seem hungry for more, we introduce "Jesus stories," a short three to five minute telling of something Jesus said or did, followed by a question to spark dialogue, like "If this Jesus story happened today, what would it look like?" Sometimes this starts as an add-on to the group, with those who want to show up early or stay late. In this movement in the journey, we often form apprentice relationships, where someone who is a little further down

> When the Spirit nudges, and people seem hungry for more, we introduce "Jesus stories," a short three to five minute telling of something Jesus said or did,

the trail reaches back to walk alongside someone where they are.

As the community deepens, it may become what, biblically speaking, we would call *koinonia*. The group has become our people, our church.

And here we often include more formal elements, like Holy Communion, baptism, Bible study, deciding together some cause we want to support and giving financially toward it.

This takes on the contextual elements of the place and people. Worship in the tattoo parlor looks different than worship in the dog park, at the EV super charger, or online in our VR headsets. But there are distinguishable elements first articulated in the Nicaean Creed as one, holy, apostolic, and catholic. We understand these historic marks as a set of four interlocking relationships:

- oneness: an inward relationship with one another

- holy: an upward relationship with God

- apostolic: an outward relationship with the world

- catholic: an ofward relationship with a connection to the wider church

When people are known and loved in a deep way, worshiping a God of love that is transfiguring us to become people of love, sharing that inexhaustible love more fully with others, and deepening relationships with other faith traditions, we say: there is church! Or our minimal ecclesiology is in the words of Jesus, "Where two or more are gathered in my name, there I am in the midst." Here we have entered into the space of sanctifying grace, a life of holy love, and embodied compassion.

The final movement is when someone in the group feels a call to start another new expression. It might be a new group entirely, multiplying what we are doing, or doing something similar in a new place. Or someone in the inherited congregation catches a vision for some other new expression of faith and takes a step toward listening to new people in a new place. The loving first journey is the method to our mission as we grow in the life of grace.

The Ministry

An Old Treasure

With the mindset, message, movement, and method treasures before us, we are at a place where a look at the ministry treasure of Methodism is in order. It is fair to say that it emerged out of the monastic model, especially Third-Order monasticism. We explore this historic ministry in its own right because it is here where we see what John Wesley's phrase "the people called Methodist" meant.

First, it meant a plurality of people. Men and women. Laity and clergy. Young and old. Christians and seekers. Rich and poor. Educated and illiterate. Leaders and followers. They all came together in Methodism. It was not an ideal or stress-free community. But it was authentic in the sense that everyone was a beloved child of God, made in God's image, with the capacity to grow in grace in terms of loving God, others, and themselves.

Second, it was a passionate people. The only requirement was to have a "desire to flee the wrath to come." We don't talk like that today. We would instead describe it as being sick and tired of being sick and tired (Matthew 11:28). We would call it abandoning self-salvation efforts and seeking to live God's way (Matthew 5:3). We would say it's "deciding to follow Jesus, no turning back, no turning back" (Mark 1:17). Everyone began at a different place but with the common purpose of becoming devoted disciples of Christ.

Third, it meant a patterned people. With a vision of holiness of heart and life, Methodists practiced the means of grace that conformed them to the image of Christ—inwardly by the works of piety[1] and outwardly by the works of mercy.[2] These means—that is, commu-

---

1.   Elaine Heath, *Five Means of Grace* (Abingdon Press, 2017) and Paul W. Chilcote, ed., *The Wesleyan Tradition: A Paradigm for Renewal* (Abingdon Press, 2002), chapter 6.

2.   Chilcote, *The Wesleyan Tradition: A Paradigm for Renewal*, chapter 7.

nion and compassion—were seen in the life and ministry of Jesus himself, moving John Wesley to call him the Christian's pattern.[3]

Fourth, it meant a proactive people. Here is where the Third-Order ministry of Methodism is seen. The people called Methodist were uncloistered, fanning out all over the place to live their lives for Christ, doing so within the natural roles they carried out every day. Methodist ministry was the practice of ordinary holiness, what Brother Lawrence described as "doing little things for God" in his classic *The Practice of the Presence of God.*

All of this came together in the Annual Conference, where Minutes were produced in relation to three intentions: what to teach, how to teach, and what to do.[4] The Minutes created what John Wesley often called "The Connection,"[5] giving them their marching orders for the coming year. No matter where they were, the Minutes provided a sense of oneness and purpose. It was an expression of life together across Methodism.

If you have noticed an absence of differentiation between laity and clergy in this description of ministry,

---

3. This is why Thomas a Kempis's book *The Imitation of Christ* was so important to him, and one of the first things he published in an abridged edition in 1735 entitled, *The Christian's Pattern.*

4. *The Works of John Wesley,* volume 10, edited by Henry D. Rack (Abingdon Press, 2011).

5. Steve writes about this in his book, *Prayer and Devotional Life of United Methodists* (Abingdon Press, 1999), chapter 3.

If you have noticed an absence of differentiation between laity and clergy in this description of ministry, we are glad. we are glad. The distinction was minimized in Methodism. Like other renewal movements, it was largely a laity enterprise. The clergy served liturgical and sacramental functions, but overall they served alongside the laity in ministry, which can be described in the following ways.

Ministry was apostolic. The verbs used to describe it make this clear: *spread*, *offer*, and *go* to name a few. The Methodists incarnated the spirit of the first apostles, understanding that they were "sent ones" into the world in Jesus's name. They had a go-to mentality, not a come-to one. They lived with the Great Commission as their mandate and the Wind of the Spirit as their power.

The beginning of the Methodist Episcopal Church in 1784 was consequence of apostolic ministry begun nearly twenty years earlier when John sent the first Methodist missionaries to the colonies, with the exhortation to "offer them Christ." This was the same vision that had fueled the growth of Methodism in Great Britain.

Ministry was vocational.[6] Methodists ministered largely within the contexts of their lives. In the monastic spirit they blended prayer and work in the crucible of their roles and tasks. They understood ministry in the sense described in Sirach: "Their work is their prayer; their prayer is their work" (Sirach 38:39, *The Message Bible*).[7]

This comes through most clearly in letters John Wesley wrote, helping people live their faith through their accustomed roles and responsibilities. But he also wrote treatises to particular people (e.g., "Advice to a Soldier") that gave them counsel. This is a testimony to the naturalness of ministry that uses us according to our temperaments and talents.

Ministry was communal. Methodism eschewed "holy solitaries" ("me-and-Jesus" spirituality) and designed almost every aspect of its ministry to be an expression of life together. John Wesley believed that personal experiences should be shared (the same day if possible) in what he called religious talk.[8]

---

6.   Paul W. Chilcote, *John Wesley Speaks on Christian Vocation* (Cascade Books, 2001).

7.   This is *The Message Bible: Catholic Ecumenical Edition* (ACTA Publications, 2013).

8.   He used the abbreviation RT in his diary to indicate when he engaged in it. An example of moving from personal experience to life together was when he read William Law in his morning devotions, and in the afternoon wrote "RT Law" in his diary.

> Unless and until we tell others what we have seen and heard, in the spirit of the apostles (Acts 4:20), we cannot know how our experience connects with and enriches someone else.

Wesley would surely have agreed with Frederick Buechner's belief "the story of any one of us is in some way the story of us all."[9] But unless and until we tell others what we have seen and heard, in the spirit of the apostles (Acts 4:20), we cannot know how our experience connects with and enriches someone else. Here is another reason that holy conferencing was named among the means of grace in Methodism.

Ministry was pastoral. Charles lived that as a parish priest; John lived it as the abbot of a Third Order movement.[10] The pastoral spirit and form of the brothers became the intent of Methodists to "watch over one another in love." They did it in their groups, in home visitation, and in spiritual guidance.

---

9.   Frederick Buechner, *The Sacred Journey* (Harper & Row, 1982), 6.

10.   Martin Schmidt, *John Wesley: A Theological Biography*, volume 2, part 2 (Abingdon Press, 1973), chapter 8, "John Wesley as Pastor."

The pastoral nature of Methodism extended beyond their caregiving to each other, moving into their compassion for strangers. The *General Rules of the United Societies* enjoined the Methodists to care for "the souls and bodies" of people. The weekly collection was given to fund works of mercy in society. Ministry was pastoral from start to finish.

With this theology of ministry, it is no stretch to find Methodism expressive of practical divinity. It is the old treasure that reminds us that we have not embraced the faith until we live it.

A New Treasure

The new ministry treasure that sparkles from within the old chest today looks like diversity, lay empowerment, a recovery of the sacredness of all work, a universal priesthood, purposeful discipleship, a commitment to inclusion, the communitarian impulse, and a shared value to watch over one another in love.

One can see in the plurality of fresh expressions a wide array of people, cultures, modes, and theologies. These expressions of church are as diverse as the people who make them their spiritual home, the places where they meet, the times when they gather, and the practices that bring them together.

Consider just a snapshot of the congregations Jill and I (Michael) lead. On Saturday mornings, Connect gathers kids and families in the Martin Luther King Jr. Center of Wildwood, for pancakes, arts and crafts, Jesus stories, and play. Across town, a group circles up in Bark Park to share in a spiritual devotion as their dogs run and play at Paws of Praise. On Sunday afternoon, Tattoo Church gathers in Beauty in a Canvas parlor for tattoo talks, fresh ink, and Holy Communion.

Monday nights, around fifty residents gather in the chemical dependency unit of the local rehab for Higher Power Hour, which includes prayer, worship, and an open share discussion. Following that, a group gathers in Tijuana Flats for Burritos and Bibles. Tuesdays, a group for senior saints called Shenanigans gathers in the Brookdale Assisted Living Community. On Wednesdays, folks show up with mats and foam blocks to engage in a spiritual conversation followed by a yoga flow. One Saturday evening a month, EV enthusiasts gather at the Tesla Supercharger to prayerfully discuss ecotheology and creation care.

Compassion UMC in Ocala is a blended ecology church plant that includes women's sober housing, a Tuesday night community dinner, and a small Sunday worshiping community of primarily women in recovery.

St. Marks UMC Ocala, a congregation that was almost closed in 2020, now has a Wednesday night community dinner called Family Table, in which around one hundred folks gather for a shared meal, art, and testimony. Eat. Pray. Play. is a gathering for children and families who need childcare during 12 step meetings. On Sunday, another hundred people gather for three worship experiences, Fresh Worship (in between a fresh expression and contemporary worship), Recovery Church (an experience that features a Jesus story and 12 step discussion), and Vintage Worship (a traditional service). Living Room Church VR gathers in the Metaverse to worship as avatars in headsets.

Each of these micro-communities are led by lay leaders. The communities they start flow from their passion. The motivation is not extrinsic, something someone is telling them to do, but rather intrinsic, flowing from their own heart.

These examples come from just a single cooperative parish, churches cooperating to nurture fresh expressions. Imagine if every Christian and every congregation committed to cultivate just one new expression of church for people who don't do church!

Each of these micro-communities are led by lay leaders. The communities they start flow from their passion. The motivation is not extrinsic, something someone is telling them to do, but rather intrinsic, flowing from their own heart. This is what Henri Nouwen meant when he said, "For the minister is called to recognize the sufferings of his own time in his own heart and make that recognition the starting point of his service."[11] These communities are pushing against the false dichotomy of the sacred/secular divide. They are reclaiming the idea that all space and all people are sacred, not just the cathedrals and the people who gather in them.

The pattern these communities take are synchronized with the normal rhythms of life. These lay leaders are not adding more things to their already busy lives like churches often ask us to do. They are considering the things they already do every week, with the people they already do them with, and dreaming about how that activity could become a new form of church. They are simultaneously seeking to embody the compassion of Jesus in their everyday lives.

This is a proactive and focused life of discipleship. I often hear younger folks in the inherited church say things like "What's the point?" Being a Christian feels like playing golf with no clubs: we wander around the

---

11. Henri J. Nouwen, *The Wounded Healer: Ministry in Contemporary Society* (Doubleday, 1990), xvi.

course for a while, get bored, then decide to take a hike. Or we are playing basketball with no hoop—we dribble around for a bit, then merge into the stands and get discipled by our chosen news network. In

> We have a clear goal, to grow in love for God and neighbor, and create communal habitats where others can experience that love.

fresh expressions, every person is in ministry. We have a clear goal, to grow in love for God and neighbor, and create communal habitats where others can experience that love.

So, they are by nature apostolic, a "sent" form of church. We are not twiddling our thumbs behind the stained-glass, hoping people show up. We go out as little teams actively following the Spirit into the world. Locating the "persons of peace" who welcome us to their table, breaking bread, doing life together. As people mature in these communities, the built-in assumption is that each one of us will start our own little community with people we love and care for. We are shifting from playing host to learning to be good guests again. The way Jesus taught the disciples (Luke 10:1-9).

In this we are reclaiming the idea of a universal priesthood. Following Jesus is a vocational endeavor; consider the Latin origin *vocationem,* literally "a calling," related to *vox*, the "voice." It is a whole life choice. We cannot compartmentalize our faith in a one-hour service on Sundays. This is in fact what so many "nones and dones" are pushing against. Sociological research has demonstrated that regular church attendance does not positively correlate with increased compassion response.[12] If we go to church our entire lives and are still racist, homophobic, and downright mean, what does this communicate to non-Christians? Where is the fruit of the Spirit? Every person is a priest, ordained in the waters of our baptism to the ministry of reconciliation.

This commitment is lived out communally. Sociologist Robin Williams (1965) famously identified the core values of US society: achievement and success, individualism, hard work, efficiency and practicality, material comfort, and freedom, to name a few.[13] These are values of an individualistic culture. Surgeon General Murthy suggests these values that dominate modern culture elevate the narrative of rugged individualist and the pur-

---

12. As early as the 1960s studies began to indicate church attendance does not positively correlate with increased social compassion (Lenski, 1961; Glock and Stark, 1965; Allport and Ross, 1967; Rokeach, 1969a, 1969b; Christenson, 1976; Ai, Amy L., and Monika Ardelt, *Role of Faith in the Well-Being of Older Adults: Linking Theories with Evidence in an Interdisciplinary Inquiry* [Nova Science Publishers, 2009]).

13. Robin Williams, Jr., *American Society: A Sociological Interpretation*, 2nd ed. (Knopf, 1965).

suit of self-determination might be contributing to the epidemic of loneliness.[14]

Those individualistic values also contrast with collectivistic culture. Consider the African anthropological framework of *ubuntu*. The concept of ubuntu highlights the interdependency of humanity. All individuals are woven together in a single interconnected organism, so that even a small act of love impacts the entire world.

Ubuntu emphasizes that a person is a person through other persons. One person's humanity is inextricably linked in a bundle of life with all others. We are who we are through others, and we need to be in relationship with those others in a way that brings healing to us all.

Fresh expressions are countercultural in this way. We value the greater good of the community over the preferences of the individual. We do ministry in teams, and we seek to encourage one another in a life of love. Or as John Wesley said, "The gospel of Christ knows of no religion, but social; no holiness but social holiness. Faith working by love, is the length and breadth and depth and height of Christian perfection."[15]

This means these communities are pastoral, but perhaps not in the conventional sense. It is not the respon-

---

14. Vivek Murthy, *Together: The Healing Power of Human Connection in a Sometimes Lonely World* (Harper Wave, 2020), 13.

15. John Wesley, *Hymns and Sacred Poems* (1739), preface, page viii.

We do this in a mode of shared leadership that is more a circle than a pyramid. sibility of a single shepherd to be the personal spiritual butler of a flock. It is a community of people who watch over one another in love. We do this in a mode of shared leadership that is more a circle than a pyramid. Every person in the group is expected to seek to do good and do no harm. This means we encourage the best in each other and call each other out when our behavior seems harmful to ourselves and others.

Doing life together in this way is difficult. Isolation is easy. Community is hard. It fights against our impulses and the larger societal forces de-forming us toward consumerism, individualism, and narcissism. But it is the most rewarding way to live. The full life, the eternal life, the life that is truly life.

The Milieu

An Old Treasure

Another important treasure in early Methodism is its milieu—that is, the atmosphere and environment in which it was born and grew. The milieu treasure shares characteristics with the mindset one, but is a term to describe two key external factors: Methodism's place and time.

With respect to place, we see it in John Wesley's declaration to his bishop that "I look upon the world as my parish." He had been doing so for years in ministries he conducted with fellow members of the Holy Club at

Oxford, as a missionary in Georgia, and in events leading up to his bishop's remonstrance. There's no doubt that his sense of place emerged from Jesus's example, as he cared for those whom organized religion had marginalized and oppressed. And as the Wesleys would surely have affirmed, Jesus's conduct became his commission (Matthew 28:19).

Location is one indication we understand that ministry is not only deep but also wide. Methodism located itself in the "highways and hedgerows" where Jesus told his disciples to go. And it set up shop in places underserved by both the church and the state.

When time and place were combined, the Wesleys ministered with a threefold conviction: everyone is open to God sometime, no one is open to God all the time, some people are open to God now.

With respect to time, Charles Wesley named it in his hymn *A Charge to Keep* in the phrase "to serve the present age." That, he wrote, is the way we live where the I AM God is, and where we are called to minister. It is actually the only time there is for (as Charles went on to write) engaging all our powers to do our Master's will.

When time and place were combined, the Wesleys ministered with a threefold conviction: everyone is open to God sometime; no one is open to God all the time; some people are open to God now. They went in search of the "now" people, and when finding them, thye invited them into the life of Christian disciples under the nurture of Methodist resources.

On paper, this looks not only well and good but also obvious. In practice it was more challenging, and the pushback came most vehemently by the political and religious leaders, who had a different view of place and time than the Wesleys did. The challenges forced them on numerous occasions to answer the question, "Shall we obey people, or God?" To the best of their ability, they answered, "God."

> The milieu of Methodism was counter-intuitive and counter-cultural because it operated in relation to the reign of God, not the kingdoms of this world.

The milieu of Methodism was counter-intuitive and counter-cultural because it operated in relation to the reign of God, not the kingdoms of this world. With that intention guiding and couraging them, they accepted the persecution Jesus said would come to his followers (Matthew 5:10-12).

Methodists learned the difference between disobedience and dissent, and they chose the way of dissent by their commitment to a different place and operating with a different sense of time than "the principalities and powers" did.

Disobedience (which is what the Methodists were accused of) is the rejection of human laws (political and religious) deemed unjust. Dissent (which was the style of Methodism) is the adherence to divine laws deemed just.[1] In other words, Methodism moved in relation to what it was for, not what it was against. This did not forestall the ire of opponents, but it did provide Methodists with a purity of heart (Matthew 5:8) that moved them to be merciful (Matthew 5:7) as they sought the things "which are above" (Colossians 3:1-4). The ministry of Methodism was grounded in this milieu.

A New Treasure

I (Michael) recently experienced an odd juxtaposition of an evening. One of our congregations, Compassion UMC mentioned earlier, is a church plant. We inherited the building of a previous congregation that had closed.

---

1.   Divine laws are summed up in specific passages (e.g., Micah 6:8, Matthew 22:34-40, Acts 10–15, and Galatians 3:28 and 5:22-23). In today's language we call them the ethics of love and justice, values that ignite actions of fairness, equity, inclusion, and the advancement of the common good.

Another group used the facility for a time, then disaffili-
ated from the UMC. Our board met to go over bids for
a renovation to turn the building into a women's recovery housing center. We would need to raise $600,000 to
complete the renovation. As that meeting was conclud-
ing, friends from our community dinner began to come
in early for the meal and to charge their tech devices.
Ninety percent of the attendees are experiencing home-
lessness or are living in nearby half-way houses. So we
needed to raise over half a million dollars, with people
who have no homes, assets, or even a dollar to give? Help
us, Jesus!

I wondered if I was not standing in a moment of
juxtaposition that leapt backward to the heart of our
tradition. The Methodist movement was formed in the
crucible of a society plagued with suffering and injustice.
Len Sweet describes the milieu in terms of being one of
the worst crime waves in English history.[2] There was mas-
sive inequality and exploitation. Fifty-five percent of children died before age five. There was an alehouse for every
twenty households. London was the sex worker capital of
the world. Alcoholism, gambling, prostitution, degrading
sports, and a socially disengaged church were normal.[3]

---

2.   Leonard Sweet, *Me and We: God's New Social Gospel* (Abingdon, 2014), 33.

3.   Leonard Sweet, *The Greatest Story Never Told: Revive Us Again*
(Abingdon, 2012), 86

Yet it was right in the heartbeat of the pain that the people called Methodists became an incarnational presence. Among the masses of uneducated working class— in the miners' camps, debtors' prisons, and street corners where the people lived—a movement from the edge was born. The Wesleys were known to frequent disreputable spots, among those of questionable character. John Wesley earned a reputation as the "pastor of the mob." He wrote, "I bear the rich and love the poor, therefore I spend almost all of my time with them."[4] The Wesleys did ministry amid the sore spots of English society. They worked against electoral corruption; structured systematic distribution of food, medicine, clothing, and loans; and organized temporary employment for the destitute.[5]

Preceding the global pandemic that took our breath away, we were facing the multiple and interconnected pandemics of systemic racism, inequality, poverty, climate change, political extremism, corrupt justice systems, an increase in mental illness, and the largest overdose epidemic in the history of the US.

Shelly Rambo, a theologian who works in the discipline of trauma studies suggests that in our contemporary setting, PTSD is no longer only a diagnostic label for individuals in a suffering condition, rather "it

---

4. Wesley, *Letters*, vol. iv, p. 266. To Ann Foard, 29th September, 1764.

5. Sweet, *Me and We*, 33.

has become a way of naming the conditions of life more broadly."[6] Unresolved trauma spills out in patterns of harm and can be passed on generationally. We live in a traumatized age. These are all features of the epidemic of loneliness and isolation we described earlier.

Whereas it seems a tendency of some churches has been to hunker down in the safety of our steeples, emerging movements are moving back into the heartbeat of the pain again. We see one aspect of communal life in Jesus is a clear mandate to be involved in the work of social justice. Intrinsic to the loving first journey is a commitment to move out in loving service to the world as it is, here and now. It includes not only works of mercy, caring for the throwaways of unjust systems, but seeking to dismantle the policies and structures of the injustice machine itself. There is a movement toward *doing justice together*.[7] This does indeed require us to awaken the Methodist spirit of dissent and even, at times, civil disobedience. This emerges from a spirituality of compassion—a sensitivity to suffering in self and others with a commitment to try to alleviate and prevent it.

---

6.   Stephanie N. Arel and Shelly Rambo (eds.), *Post-Traumatic Public Theology* (Palgrave Macmillan, 2016), 9.

7.   Stephanie Moore Hand and Michael Adam Beck, *Doing Justice Together: Fresh Expressions Pathways for Healing in Your Church* (Abingdon Press, 2024).

Where our institutional impulse is often self-preservation, the way of Jesus is self-donation.

Early Methodist gatherings were a great equalizer, where people of all walks of life came together as one. John Wesley would later reflect that it was the inclusive nature of the societies that he was most proud of.[8] The ultimate gift of fresh expressions of church is communal life in Jesus. Where our institutional impulse is often self-preservation, the way of Jesus is self-donation. A new Methodism should start where the old methodism did—among the marginalized, excluded, and oppressed. In communities of people who are often outside the center of wealth-generation and influence.

John Wesley taught his itinerant preachers to "search the Scriptures." . . . "Whether you like it or no, read and pray daily." But he also instructed them to "spend all the morning, or at least five hours in twenty-four, in reading the most *useful books*, and that regularly and constantly."[9] Study Scripture, and study your place and times.

The Wesleys were able to communicate the Christian faith into the dawning Industrial Society, in "plain

---

8. Laceye Warner, *Knowing Who We Are* (Abingdon Press, 2024), 17, 28.

9. Iain H. Murray, *Wesley and the Men Who Followed* (The Banner of Truth Trust, 2003), 89–90 (emphasis original).

words for plain people," harnessing the emerging technologies. They found ways to embody the church in the "world as parish" (first, second, and third places of the day). They also adapted to the rhythms of the time—consider, the 5 a.m. gatherings with miners and farmers along the road as they went to work, which Wesley called "the glory of the Methodists."[10]

Notable sociologist Manuel Castells posits that at the end of the second millennium, a new form of society arose from the interactions of several major social, technological, economic, and cultural transformations: the network society. Like in the Wesleys' day, we are in a period of historical transition between different forms of society, moving from the Industrial Age into the Information Age. The network society consists of a social structure made up of networks enabled by microelectronics-based information and communications technologies.[11]

The "fields" have changed, as we must now consider the "space of flows" (digitally built environments and technologies that enable them) and the "space of places" in a network society. Multiple layers of networks, digital and physical, intertwine, connecting people in nodes

10. Arthur S. Wood, *The Burning Heart: John Wesley, Evangelist* (Bethany Fellowship, 1978), 154.

11. Manuel Castells, *The Rise of the Network Society* (Blackwell, 2000), xvii–xviii.

and hubs, which we have referred to as the first, second, and third places of local communities. These are the new "fields" of the Information Age.

A new Methodism is once again adapting to the milieu of a traumatized age in the emerging social structure of the network society, offering the gift of communal life in Jesus to a lonely world.

The Mission

An Old Treasure

In every one of the preceding treasures, we have seen an expressed or implied missiology. But we must explore it specifically to round out the vision and intent we have for this book.

We begin with Jesus who taught that if much has been given to us, much will be required of us (Luke 12:48). To describe this in eucharistic language, we are taken, blessed, broken, and given.[1] *Mission* is the one-word summary of a eucharistic life.

But closer to the Wesleys' day, their commitment to mission was influenced by their experience with Quietism. It was a belief among some Christians who held that they were only supposed to do what the Spirit prompted them to do. They were to move only when they were moved. At first glance, it sounded "spiritual," but in actual practice, it undermined almost everything having to do with ministry. At the extreme, certain Quietists would not even receive the Lord's Supper unless they felt moved to do so.

The Wesleys rejected this kind of piety, believing that whatever we have been told to do in Scripture is the primal prompting of the Spirit, which needs no additional prompting. In this sense, mission is enacting the will of God through intention, not emotion. And with this conviction the Methodists engaged in mission, which has been described in three movements.

First, Methodist mission reached the unreached. Externally, this meant going where such people were. It meant going there to love, listen, learn, and live together. Internally, it meant practicing hospitality when any unreached people sought them out. In either aspect,

---

1.   Henri Nouwen has written of this eucharistic pattern in his book *Life of the Beloved* (Crossroad, 1992).

acceptance was the hallmark. Theologically, Methodist mission practiced unconditional love.

Second, Methodist mission sought to renew the Church. We have already described Methodism as an *ecclesiola en ecclesia*—a little church in the big Church. With respect to mission, it was an active presence. Here is another link to monasticism. Methodism's intent was to take "what is" and make it better. Methodism's ecumenical constituency enabled it to engage in that effort in more than one ecclesial body.

Third, Methodist mission aimed to reform the nation. The vocational ministry, we have noted, meant that the people called Methodist lived all over the place and worked in every facet of society. Here again is why being a lay movement made national reform possible in ways that would not have been possible by clergy. Laypersons were the very kinds of salt and light Jesus spoke about in the Sermon on the Mount (Matthew 5:13-16), a mission carried out by laity through the rest of the New Testament era, and for another two hundred years.[2]

Mission is the launch pad for the Christian witness. And when combined with the other treasures we have described, it is a mission that enables us to say that, like

---

2. In making Christianity the official religion of the Roman empire in 313 CE, it became imperialized, one unfortunate result being the clericalization of the Church.

our predecessors, we have been obedient to the heavenly vision.

A New Treasure

The new methodism of the twenty-first century is once again a movement in the fields. In fresh expressions, we are crystal clear about our purpose "to reach new people, in new places, and in new ways." We are seeking to cultivate communal life in Jesus with people not currently connected to any church.

We hold to four missional values that serve as a kind of compass for our journey. The communities we seek to cultivate are:

Inclusive: a manifestation of God's outreaching love; a place of healing, not harm; an environment of grace, a belonging before believing space where all are welcome and where the "good news" is good for all and made available to all (Luke 4:18-19). The community exists primarily for people not currently connected to any church.

Accessible: meaning close, culturally appropriate, and speaking the common language(s) of the context. This value was embodied by Jesus in the incarnation when he came and "made his dwelling among us" (John 1:14 NIV).

Transfiguring: where we acknowledge the innate "very goodness" in every person and understand how each of us are on a journey of renewal. We can be honest about our wounds, challenges, and the progress of our spiritual growth in a community of love and grace. We are free to process our discipleship journey in an unfiltered and prayerful way that brings real healing (James 5:16). This empowers us for works of mercy and justice in our communities.

Connectional: Methodist fresh expressions exist in a relationship with each other and the wider church. They assume the emerging social structure of the network society in a digital age. This connectionalism resembles the nature of the early church and is particularly evident in the relationship between Jerusalem and Antioch (Acts 15).

We can see deep synergy in these values with the three movements of Methodist mission: a movement toward the unreached, a movement to renew the church, and a movement to reform the nation.

The inclusive nature of these communities is simply another way to talk about mission. From the graceful garden call, "Where are you?" (Genesis 3:9), through the Abrahamic promise that all the families of the earth shall be blessed (Genesis 12:3), to the final vision of the great multitude that none could count gathered before the throne (Revelation 7:9), God's intent is to wrap all of humanity in everlasting love. The church is a missional instrument in the hand of God to accomplish this work.

The Wesleyan impulse to go out into the world seems to get lost sometimes, as if the church is suffering with a case of apostolic amnesia. As noted earlier, we have defaulted to a "come to us" mode of mission. But the attractional church is simply inaccessible to so many people. Any time we choose to meet at a particular time, place, and way, it will be accessible to some people but inaccessible to any who can't come at that time, to that place, and to whom our way may be foreign.

> The church needs to be taken, blessed, broken, and given. Churches springing up in every nook and cranny of life, at many times throughout the week, become more accessible to more people.

The only way the church will become more accessible is through this eucharistic understanding of mission. The church needs to be taken, blessed, broken, and given. Churches springing up in every nook and cranny of life, at many times throughout the week, become more accessible to more people.

The transfiguring nature of these communities communicates both the awakening of the "very goodness" innately present in every person and the goodness, beauty, and truth that is baked into every molecule of creation itself. God created the world and called it "good." Goodness is literally the molecular nature of all reality. Thus, people are good, communities are good, and societal connectivity is good. And yet, every dimension of life is currently warped by sin. Sadly, this includes the church.

The good that the church has done in the world is incalculable. Christians have created the first free hospitals, fed the hungry, cared for the sick and vulnerable, and sheltered the stranger for two millennia. Yet the church, for all her beauty marks, also has blemishes. She has been hijacked to collude with colonization, genocide, slavery, racism, patriarchy, and the harm and exclusion of LGBTQ persons. One of the leading reasons for disaffiliation from organized religion among emerging generations is the harmful behavior of Christians.

This is why we believe any talk of the *missio Dei* needs to be grounded in the *passio Dei*. Whereas *missio Dei* (Latin for "mission of God") understands mission as an attribute and activity of God, and furthermore that the church is missionary by its very nature, the *passio Dei* (Latin for "passion of God") is grounded primarily in the incarnation, suffering, and crucifixion (passion) of Jesus.

The cross need not be understood as a bloodthirsty God, abusing God's son to make right our sins. It's humanity who crucifies God, not God crucifying Jesus. On the cross we encounter a traumatized and crucified God. A God who is Trinity experiences that suffering for us, with us, and in us.

Perhaps the passion of Jesus offers a corrective to the ways the missional church conversation has gone astray. Missional describes what God is about, passional describes how God goes about it.

The passion most fully reveals God's nature, the self-emptying (*kenotic*), other-oriented, and sacrificial love fully displayed in the crucifixion. The passion of Christ expresses God's inhabitation of human vulnerability and suffering. Perhaps the passion of Jesus offers a corrective to the ways the missional church conversation has gone astray. Missional describes what God is about; passional describes how God goes about it. We get to participate in the mission of God, but we must do so in the way of Jesus.

Mission has at times become disconnected from the compassion of Christ. The great commandment (love God and neighbor) comes before the great commission (go make disciples). We wonder if at times the church has gotten this backwards.

John Wesley referred to Methodism as a "religion of the heart." Overemphasis on *orthodoxy* ("right opinion/belief") or *orthopraxy* ("right practice"), to the neglect of *orthokardia* ("right heart") can lead to the "hard heartedness" that Jesus confronted in the religious leadership of his day (Mark 3:5). Further, we think an approach to mission that disregards *orthopathy* ("right pathos/suffering," i.e., experience of God), can and has caused harm.

We cannot rightly emphasize sanctification (humanity re-conformed to the *imago Dei*, image of God) as the ultimate completion of the *missio Dei* unless we embrace the kenotic way of Jesus, *passio Dei*.

Pathos includes thinking, feeling, and behavior but grounds it in compassionate *being-with*. It's about normalizing the experience of Jesus's compassion in our own missional approach. We want to remind the church that mission flows from the loving heart of God. Its origin is the compassion of God. This reconnects head, heart, and hands—a distinctly Wesleyan vision of mission.

Fresh expressions can have a transfiguring effect on society as a whole. Some are implicitly created to "reform the nation" by taking up the work of antiracism, prison reform, poverty alleviation, and full LGBTQ inclusion. Some organize grassroots mobilization that seeks change at the level of policy making and law.

Others have a more subtle effect. As we offer communal life in Jesus in a society aching with isolation, people find healing. Those who once considered themselves "addicted and afflicted" find recovery. Those in a pattern of suicidal ideation find friends and a purpose for life. People who are digitally hyperconnected but utterly alone find a balm for their loneliness. Healthy people are the basic building block of a healthy society. As people are formed in the compassion of Jesus, they can help awaken society to the goodness that is already there.

Conclusion

THIS LITTLE BOOK ENDS with a big question: "What would treasured renewal look like where you are? In your life, your group, your congregation?" It is the question we must ask if the book is to achieve its aim to inform and inspire long-haul renewal at the local level.

Neither the old treasures nor the new ones that we have named fully describe the Wesleyan tradition. To do that would require a much longer book, and in some ways (given the richness and diversity of the tradition) it is an impossible task. The ones we have chosen are key elements that need to be preserved and perpetuated. And in this time of New Awakening, we must "engage ourselves unto the Lord" (Covenant Renewal Service) here and now.

We must run with determination the course laid out for us (Hebrews 12:1). And, like our predecessors in the faith, that means laying down some weights (unnecessary obstacles) along with sins that have eroded our internal life and external witness.

We leave you with the question above because we trust that the Spirit will be at work among any who ask, seek, and knock with the resolve to find and follow God's will. We pray that you will be among them, individually and in your faith communities, being persuaded now as then, "The best of all is, God is with us!"

Related Readings

This book is a primer, a door opener into a larger house. It is meant to ignite a deeper and wider exploration of ecclesial change.

The footnotes are the place to begin because they most directly link you to resources that attend the treasured-renewal intent of this book. In addition, the following related readings are also recommended. The list is short in order not to overwhelm you.

The works cited below blend old and new treasures just as this book does, but we have arranged them into the two dimensions of renewal that we have emphasized.

Old-Treasure Resources

Chilcote, Paul W., *Cultivating Christlikeness: Loving as Jesus Loved* (Abingdon Press, 2024).

Chilcote, Paul W. and Steve Harper, *Upward! Wesleyan Formation in Three Movements* (Abingdon Press, 2023).

Harper, Steve, *Devotional Life in Wesleyan Tradition: A Workbook* (Upper Room Books, 1995).

Harper, Steve, *Life in Christ: The Core of Intentional Spirituality* (Abingdon Press, 2020).

Harper, Steve, *The Way to Heaven: The Gospel According to John Wesley* (Zondervan, 2003)

Maddox, Randy, *Radical Grace: John Wesley's Practical Theology* (Kingswood Books, 1994).

Heath, Elaine A. and Larry Duggins, *Missional, Monastic, Mainline* (Cascade Books, 2014).

Oliveto, Karen, *Together at the Table: Diversity without Division in The United Methodist Church* (WJK, 2018).

Sweet, Leonard, *11 Genetic Gateways to Spiritual Awakening* (Abingdon Press, 1998).

Warner, Laceye C., *Knowing Who We Are: The Wesleyan Way of Grace* (Abingdon Press, 2024).

New-Treasure Works

Baker, Jonny and Cathy Ross, *The Pioneer Gift: Explorations in Mission* (Canterbury, 2014).

Beck, Michael Adam, *An Ecumenical Field Guide to Fresh Expressions* (Abingdon Press, 2024).

Beck, Michael Adam, and Tyler Kleeberger, *Fresh Expressions of the Rural Church* (Abingdon Press, 2022).

Beck, Michael Adam and Rosario Picardo, *Fresh Expressions in a Digital Age* (Abingdon Press, 2021).

Carter, Ken and Michael Beck, *Gardens in the Desert: How an Adaptive Church Can Lead to a Whole New Life* (Abingdon Press, 2024).

Boff, Leonardo, *Ecclesiogenesis: The Base Communities Reinvent the Church* (Orbis, 1986).

Cray, Graham, *Mission-Shaped Church: Church Planting and Fresh Expressions in a Changing Context* (Seabury Books, 2010).

Moore Hand, Stephanie, and Michael Adam Beck, *Doing Justice Together: Fresh Expressions Pathways for Healing in Your Church* (Abingdon Press, 2024).

Moynagh, Michael and Michael Beck, *The 21st Century Christian: Following Jesus Where Life Happens* (Higher Life Press, 2021).

Sweet, Leonard and Michael Beck, *Contextual Intelligence: Unlocking the Ancient Secret to Frontline Mission* (Higher Life Publishing, 2020).

www.ingramcontent.com/pod-product-compliance
Lightning Source LLC
LaVergne TN
LVHW030250250125
801924LV00005B/25